Author's Note

This book features 100 influential and
inspiring quotes by Voltaire.
Undoubtedly, this collection will give you
a huge boost of inspiration.

D1522403

1

"The most important decision you make is to be in a good mood."

2

"Despite the enormous quantity of books, how few people read! And if one reads profitably, one would realize how much stupid stuff the vulgar herd is content to swallow every day."

3

"The comfort of the rich
depends upon an abundant
supply of the poor."

4

"If God did not exist, it would be necessary to invent him."

5

"Faith consists in believing
what reason cannot."

6

"Don't think money does everything or you are going to end up doing everything for money."

7

"Every man is a creature of the age in which he lives and few are able to raise themselves above the ideas of the time."

8

"Sensual pleasure passes and vanishes, but the friendship between us, the mutual confidence, the delight of the heart, the enchantment of the soul, these things do not perish and can never be destroyed."

9

"We never live; we are always in the expectation of living."

10

"No opinion is worth burning
your neighbor for."

11

"The longer we dwell on our misfortunes, the greater is their power to harm us."

12

"Men will always be mad, and those who think they can cure them are the maddest of all."

13

"The only way to comprehend what mathematicians mean by Infinity is to contemplate the extent of human stupidity."

14

"The more often a stupidity is repeated, the more it gets the appearance of wisdom."

15

"The mirror is a worthless invention. The only way to truly see yourself is in the reflection of someone else's eyes."

16

"It is clear that the individual who persecutes a man, his brother, because he is not of the same opinion, is a monster."

"One day everything will be
well, that is our hope.
Everything's fine today, that
is our illusion."

18

"Man is free at the instant he wants to be."

19

"Animals have these advantages over man: they never hear the clock strike, they die without any idea of death, they have no theologians to instruct them, their last moments are not disturbed by unwelcome and unpleasant ceremonies, their funerals cost them nothing, and no one starts lawsuits over their wills."

20

"It is with books as with men: a very small number play a great part."

21

"Prejudices are what fools use
for reason."

"God is a comedian playing to an audience that is too afraid to laugh."

23

"The secret of being a bore is to tell everything."

24

"Fools have a habit of believing that everything written by a famous author is admirable. For my part I read only to please myself and like only what suits my taste."

"It is better to risk saving a guilty person than to condemn an innocent one."

26

"God is a circle whose center is everywhere and circumference nowhere."

"Appreciation is a wonderful thing. It makes what is excellent in others belong to us as well."

28

"The human brain is a complex organ with the wonderful power of enabling man to find reasons for continuing to believe whatever it is that he wants to believe."

"Cherish those who seek the truth but beware of those who find it."

"It is not enough to conquer;
one must learn to seduce."

"I have never made but one prayer to God, a very short one: Oh Lord, make my enemies ridiculous. And God granted it."

32

"If this is the best of possible worlds, what then are the others?"

"History never repeats itself.
Man always does."

34

"The infinitely small have a pride infinitely great."

35

"The pursuit of pleasure must be the goal of every rational person."

36

"Marriage is the only adventure open to the cowardly."

"One merit of poetry few persons will deny: it says more and in fewer words than prose."

38

"If you want good laws, burn those you have and make new ones."

"A State can be no better than the citizens of which it is composed. Our labour now is not to mould States but make citizens."

"May God defend me from my friends: I can defend myself from my enemies."

41

"He must be very ignorant for
he answers every question he
is asked."

42

"Our labour preserves us from three great evils — weariness, vice, and want."

43

"Men are equal; it is not birth but virtue that makes the difference."

"I would rather obey a fine lion, much stronger than myself, than two hundred rats of my own species."

45

"Behind every successful man stands a surprised mother-in-law."

"Meditation is the dissolution
of thoughts in Eternal
awareness or Pure
consciousness without
objectification, knowing
without thinking, merging
finitude in infinity."

47

"Dare to think for yourself."

48

"We are rarely proud when we are alone."

"To succeed in the world it is not enough to be stupid – one must also be polite."

"It is an infantile superstition of the human spirit that virginity would be thought a virtue and not the barrier that separates ignorance from knowledge."

51

"Injustice in the end produces independence."

52

"To hold a pen is to be at war."

53

"When he to whom one speaks does not understand, and he who speaks himself does not understand, that is metaphysics."

"Of all religions, the Christian should of course inspire the most tolerance, but until now Christians have been the most intolerant of all men."

55

"I should like to lie at your feet
and die in your arms."

"Such then is the human condition, that to wish greatness for one's country is to wish harm to one's neighbors."

"I have lived eighty years of life and know nothing for it, but to be resigned and tell myself that flies are born to be eaten by spiders and man to be devoured by sorrow."

58

"It is as impossible to translate poetry as it is to translate music."

59

"I am the best-natured
creature in the world, and yet
I have already killed three,
and of these three two were
priests."

60

"I cannot imagine how the clockwork of the universe can exist without a clockmaker."

"Wherever my travels may lead, paradise is where I am."

"One great use of words is to hide our thoughts."

63

"What can you say to a man who tells you he prefers obeying God rather than men, and that as a result he's certain he'll go to heaven if he cuts your throat?"

64

"If you have two religions in
your land, the two will cut
each other's throats; but if
you have thirty religions,
they will dwell in peace."

"Madness is to think of too many things in succession too fast, or of one thing too exclusively."

66

"It is not inequality which is the real misfortune, it is dependence."

"The discovery of what is true and the practice of that which is good are the two most important aims of philosophy."

68

"Men argue. Nature acts."

"In every province, the chief occupations, in order of importance, are lovemaking, malicious gossip, and talking nonsense."

70

"Reading nurtures the soul, and an enlightened friend brings it solace."

71

"Is politics nothing other than
the art of deliberately lying?"

72

"Doctors put drugs of which they know little into bodies of which they know less for diseases of which they know nothing at all."

"All men are born with a nose and ten fingers, but no one was born with a knowledge of God."

74

"All the reasonings of men are not worth one sentiment of women."

75

"All is for the best in the best of possible worlds."

76

"My soul is the mirror of the universe, and my body is its frame."

"The interest I have to believe a thing is no proof that such a thing exists."

"Uncertainty is an uncomfortable position. But certainty is an absurd one."

"If we do not find anything very pleasant, at least we shall find something new."

80

"Each player must accept the cards life deals him or her; but once they are in hand, he or she alone must decide how to play the cards in order to win the game."

81

"Opinions have caused more ills than the plague or earthquakes on this little globe of ours."

"When it is a question of money, everybody is of the same religion."

83

"Our wretched species is so made that those who walk on the well-trodden path always throw stones at those who are showing a new road."

84

"It is said that God is always on the side of the big battalions."

85

"A witty saying proves nothing."

"The mouth obeys poorly
when the heart murmurs."

"Tears are the silent language of grief."

88

"Theology is to religion what poisons are to food."

"Life is thickly sown with thorns, and I know no other remedy than to pass quickly through them. The longer we dwell on our misfortunes, the greater is their power to harm us."

"Four thousand volumes of
metaphysics will not teach us
what the soul is."

"Being unable to make people
more reasonable, I preferred
to be happy away from them."

"In general, the art of government consists in taking as much money as possible from one party of the citizens to give to the other."

"Fools admire everything in an author of reputation."

"No problem can stand the assault of sustained thinking."

"If there's life on other planets, then the earth is the Universe's insane asylum."

"I know many books which have bored their readers, but I know of none which has done real evil."

"There is a wide difference between speaking to deceive, and being silent to be impenetrable."

98

"Men use thought only as authority for their injustice, and employ speech only to conceal their thoughts."

"The greatest consolation in life is to say what one thinks."

"Now, now my good man, this is no time to be making enemies."